The Water Cycle

by Sonia W. Black

Children's Press®
An imprint of Scholastic Inc.

Content Consultants
American Geosciences Institute

Library of Congress Cataloging-in-Publication Data Available

978-1-338-83705-6 (library binding) | 978-1-338-83706-3 (paperback)

10 9 8 7   25 26 27

Printed in the U.S.A. 40
First edition, 2023

Series produced by Spooky Cheetah Press
Book prototype and logo design by Book&Look
Page design by Kathleen Petelinsek, The Design Lab

Photos ©: 3 background and throughout: Freepik; 19 girl: Horst Sollinger/imageBROKER/Shutterstock; 25: swissmediavision/ Getty Images; 29: Ed Robeck; 30: 506 collection/Alamy Images.

All other photos © Shutterstock.

TABLE OF CONTENTS

Around and Around

The water on Earth has been here in some form since before the time of dinosaurs. And it is always moving.

Water moves through the oceans, the air, and all parts of the land. This process is called the water cycle. Let's find out how it works!

Earth's five major oceans are the Atlantic, Pacific, Indian, Arctic, and Southern.

CHAPTER I

All Kinds of Water

Water covers most of Earth's surface. The oceans are filled with salt water. Most rivers, lakes, and streams contain fresh water. These bodies of water are in liquid form. A liquid flows and can be poured.

Most of the water we use every day is fresh. We need to drink fresh water to stay healthy.

When it gets cold enough outside, liquid water freezes. It turns into ice, which is a solid. Water can also be found as a gas, called **water vapor**. Water is the only substance found naturally in all three states: liquid, solid, and gas. All of them are important to the water cycle.

Liquid water is found in the ocean. Water vapor is a gas that is found in steam. And ice is water as a solid.

Gas

Solid

Liquid

9

Water vapor is invisible. It is rising off this lake, but we cannot see it!

CHAPTER 2

Water in the Air

During the day, the sun heats the surface of Earth. This heat can change liquid water in rivers, lakes, and oceans into water vapor. This process is called **evaporation**. The water vapor can move throughout the atmosphere. It mixes with the air and rises toward the sky.

Water vapor is also made through transpiration. In this process, water underground enters the roots of plants. The water travels up the stems and into the leaves of the plants. Then it moves from the leaves into the air as water vapor.

This shows how water moves through a plant.

Clouds cover about 70 percent of Earth at all times.

Water vapor cools as it rises. It changes into tiny droplets of water and bits of ice. That process is called **condensation**. Lots and lots of these tiny water droplets and ice bits form a cloud. The clouds in the sky are not the only clouds that can form. Fog and mist are types of clouds, too.

CHAPTER 3

Falling Water

The water droplets that form a cloud grow bigger. The surrounding air cannot hold the droplets in the sky. Falling water, called **precipitation**, comes down from the clouds. When it is warm outside, the water falls as rain.

There could be millions of pounds of water in one cloud.

Do you like to splash in rain puddles?

It takes about an hour for a snowflake to leave its cloud and hit the ground.

The temperature of the air can affect precipitation. When the air is very cold, snowflakes can form. They fall as snow. Sometimes liquid water in the air freezes on its way to the ground, forming sleet or balls of ice called hail.

One of the largest hailstones ever found measured 18 inches all around. That is bigger than a softball!

CHAPTER 4

Water on Earth

Some precipitation falls right into bodies of water, such as oceans, lakes, rivers, and streams. Some precipitation falls on land. The ground takes in some of the water right away. But most becomes **runoff**, which flows downhill across the ground.

A raindrop starts out in a rounded shape. By the time it reaches the ground, it is flat like a hamburger bun.

Heat from the sun melts ice on mountaintops and turns it into liquid water. That water joins the runoff from rain.

The mud on these carrots shows that the ground underneath holds water.

Some runoff flows across the land until it empties into a body of water. But that does not always happen. Runoff also seeps into the top layer of soil, where it can get taken in by plants.

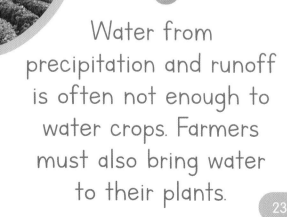

Water from precipitation and runoff is often not enough to water crops. Farmers must also bring water to their plants.

Some precipitation flows downward and sideways through spaces between soil and rocks. This water travels below the surface. It is called groundwater. The water may collect in an area underground called an aquifer. But in time, the groundwater makes its way back onto land and into rivers and oceans.

Many people get their drinking water from an aquifer.

Sometimes an aquifer has openings that allow water to flow onto the land. That is called a spring.

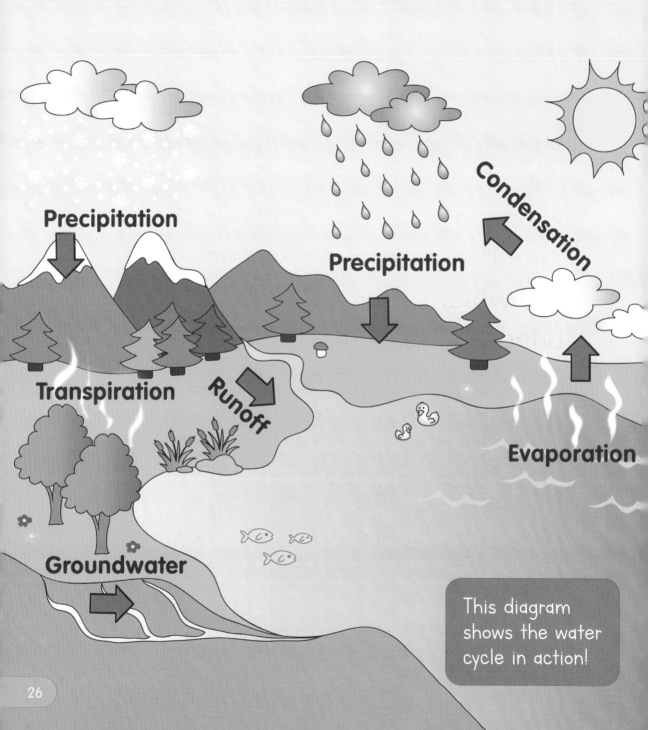

This diagram shows the water cycle in action!

Once again, heat from the sun warms the surface water. The surface water evaporates. As the water vapor cools, condensation and then precipitation can occur. The water cycle continuously brings us fresh water. It is never ending. Still, there is a limited amount of fresh water on our planet, and all living things need it to survive. This is why it is important to protect Earth's water!

TESTING TRANSPIRATION

This simple experiment will allow you to test if transpiration is happening in a plant. Start the activity in the morning or around midday so the sun will be shining for a while.

YOU WILL NEED

- An adult's help
- A leafy plant that is outside in sunlight
- A clear plastic bag, like a quart-size zip-top
- Twine or string

STEPS

1. Ask an adult to help you choose a live plant outside that will be in sunlight for a few hours.

2. Being careful not to damage the plant, place the plastic bag over a leafy part of the plant. Then use the twine or string to close the bag securely around the plant stem.

3. Visit the plant a few times over the next few hours. What do you notice on the inside of the plastic bag? Why do you think this happened?

WATER WARRIOR

MEET MARI COPENY

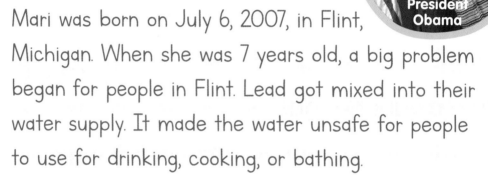
Mari with President Obama

Mari was born on July 6, 2007, in Flint, Michigan. When she was 7 years old, a big problem began for people in Flint. Lead got mixed into their water supply. It made the water unsafe for people to use for drinking, cooking, or bathing.

A year later, Mari wrote to President Obama about the problem and invited him to visit her hometown. The president met with Mari and other people in Flint. The government gave money to help the people of Flint. Today, Mari continues to work to find solutions to global problems.

GLOSSARY

condensation (kahn-den-SAY-shuhn) what happens or forms when a gas turns into a liquid

evaporation (i-va-puh-RAY-shuhn) what happens or forms when a liquid changes into a vapor or gas

precipitation (pri-sip-i-TAY-shuhn) what happens or forms when water falls from the sky in the form of rain, hail, or snow

runoff (RUHN-awf) the portion of precipitation on land that ends up in streams

water vapor (WAW-tur VAY-pur) water in the form of a gas

INDEX

ABOUT THE AUTHOR

Sonia W. Black has written many books for young readers. Ms. Black grew up in a place that is surrounded by water—the beautiful Caribbean island of Jamaica. Today, she lives in a small town in New Jersey and loves taking walks along the waterfront of Raritan Bay.